Class President

by Johanna Hurwitz

Book Guide

SCHOLASTIC
LITERACY
PLACE®

IT TAKES A LEADER
Grade 4, Unit 6

Contents

Dear Teacher,

Class President uses likeable, realistic characters to explore what it means to be a leader. Students will enjoy watching Julio's self-confidence grow as he takes an increasingly important role in helping his class solve a variety of problems. Through their reading and book conversations, students will come to appreciate Johanna Hurwitz's skill at portraying the humor and the problems that are part of everyday life.

Overview

TEACHING OPTIONS

There are many ways that students can read and enjoy *Class President*.

◆ Almost **all students** can benefit from having all or part of the book **read aloud** to help them appreciate the realistic characters and setting.

◆ A four-session plan that uses the **key strategy of Draw Conclusions** allows for both **teacher guidance** and **demonstrating independence**. This option has students read portions of the book on their own and then participate in teacher-led discussion to stimulate **meaningful conversation** and **comprehension**. See Reading the Book pages 6–10.

◆ **Cooperative groups** may work together to form **Literature Circles**. A blackline master is provided on page 11 to help students run their own successful Literature Circles.

◆ The blackline master on page 11 may also be adapted for use by students who are reading the book **in pairs** or reading **independently**.

◆ Introducing the Book, Assess Comprehension, Writing, Activities, and the Story Organizer are features of this guide that may be used with **all students**.

CONNECT TO SOURCEBOOK

Resources in the *It Takes a Leader* **Teacher's SourceBook**, such as lessons relating to the **key strategy of Draw Conclusions**, may also be adapted for use with *Class President*. In addition, each plan in the *It Takes a Leader* Teacher's Sourcebook includes specific suggestions for **linking Class President to the SourceBook literature**. Detailed suggestions are provided on pages **T50**, **T131**, and **T169** of the Teacher's SourceBook and on page **12** of this guide. Additional suggestions appear on pages T85, T215, and T255 of the Teacher's SourceBook.

JOURNAL WRITING

Throughout *Literacy Place*, students are encouraged to use journal writing to record their observations, note new vocabulary, and express their imaginations. Through journal writing, students are also encouraged to relate what they read to their own lives and to develop the skills to assess their strengths and weaknesses as readers.

Within this guide, prompts for journal writing may be found on pages 4, 5, 7, 8, 9, 10, 11, 13, and 16.

OPPORTUNITIES FOR PORTFOLIO ASSESSMENT

This guide offers a number of opportunities for portfolio assessment of both reading and writing.

READING
See pages 12–13, 16.

WRITING
See pages 13, 14–15, 16.

Introducing the Book

CREATE INTEREST

Ask students to think about famous presidents and other great leaders. Which leaders do they most admire? Why do students think these people won the elections when they ran for office? What ideas did these people stand for? Discuss that there are many different reasons that people vote for a certain candidate. Point out that this is true in every type of election. List the reasons students can think of on the chalkboard. Display the cover of *Class President,* and tell students that in the book they are about to read, a class election is very important to many of the characters in the book, especially those shown on the cover.

BUILD BACKGROUND

As the title of the book suggests, an election for class president is an important event. Invite students to consider what qualities a class president should have. What do students think a class president must be able to do? What responsibilities might a class president have? List these on the chalkboard.

```
                  Class President
        ┌──────────────────┴──────────────────┐
   Abilities                         Responsibilities
   ◆ Good Speaker                    ◆ Represent the class
   ◆ Make Decisions                     at meetings
```

DEVELOP VOCABULARY

Strategy: Synonyms and Antonyms

Throughout the book the author uses realistic dialogue and descriptions to help readers know what the characters are thinking and feeling. Write the vocabulary words on chart paper and pronounce them. Then invite volunteers to come up with synonyms and antonyms for as many of these words as they can. Record their responses. You may wish to keep this chart posted as students read. Encourage them to add more descriptive action words, with synonyms and antonyms, as they find them in the book.

Personal Word List *Class President* contains interesting words that describe actions, people, and elections. Encourage students to keep their own personal word lists for each of these categories.

Vocabulary

Organizing Concept: Descriptive Verbs

stationed: at a certain location to do a job (p. 2)

discarded: threw away (p. 13)

digesting: process of turning food one has eaten into energy, or the time and process of thinking through a new idea (p. 19)

campaigning: asking the public to vote for a certain candidate (p. 21)

chorused: said together (p. 23)

straining: working hard, using lots of attention or effort (p. 28)

shrugged: moved one's shoulders up and down (p. 42)

chided: scolded gently (p. 4)

muttered: said in a low voice (often shows discontent or worry) (p. 57)

represent: stand for; present other's point of view (p. 70)

alarmed: worried; surprised (p. 71)

PREVIEW AND PREDICT

Have students examine the cover of *Class President* and consider the clues it offers about the characters and the problem they will face in the book. You can also ask questions such as the following to help students determine a reading purpose:

◆ **Who do you think the characters on the cover of the book are?**

◆ **What problems might develop between the characters in this story?**

◆ **What might the characters have to do before the actual election for class president?**

Students may record their predictions and questions in their Journals. As they read, they can confirm or revise their predictions to see if the book is answering their questions.

ASSESSMENT

As students read the book, notice how they:

✔ make connections to the **theme** of every community having people who lead and inspire others to take action.

✔ use the **key strategy** of Draw Conclusions.

✔ recognize how understanding strategies such as **Compare/Contrast** and **Setting** adds to their appreciation of the book.

Reading On Students who are reading the book independently may read at their own pace. Other students may go on to read pages 1–21 of the book.

Meet the Author

Johanna Hurwitz says, "my parents met in a bookstore and there has never been a moment when books were not important in my life. As soon as I was old enough, I got a library card so that I would have access to even more volumes. I loved the library so much that I made the firm decision by age ten that some day I would become a librarian. I also planned that I would write books." Hurwitz fulfilled both dreams. She worked for many years as a librarian in Great Neck, New York, and is the author of more than 30 books for young readers. She has traveled all over the world talking to children about her work and has won many awards, including the Sunshine State Young Reader's Award for *Class President*. Another book about Julio and his friends, *Lucas, Class Clown*, was an IRA Children's Choice.

MORE BY JOHANNA HURWITZ

Hurray for Ali Baba Bernstein
This fourth-grader gets his nickname from his love of stories. He also has a knack for funny adventures.

President de le clase
This Spanish translation of *Class President* is just as funny as the original.

Teacher's Pet
In this earlier book in the series about Julio and his friends, Cricket is the star.

The Up and Down Spring
Bolivia is a girl whose two best friends are boys. Together the three children find a season full of adventure.

Reading the Book

This plan is divided into four sessions. Included are mini-lessons on Setting and Compare/Contrast.

Synopsis With the long hot summer finally over, fifth-grader Julio Sanchez arrives at the school yard, eager to greet his classmates. There he finds his pal Lucas Cott and super-confident Cricket Kaufman, who blurts out the news: Mrs. Upchurch, a fifth-grade teacher, has left the school. Once in class with their new teacher Mr. Flores, the children learn that they'll be electing a class president in a few weeks.

 ### LAUNCH THE KEY STRATEGY

DRAW CONCLUSIONS

THINK ALOUD It's important for me to draw conclusions, or make guesses, as I read. For example, Julio has to pretend to spend a million dollars for his arithmetic project. The first things he thinks of buying are new cars for his mother and two older brothers. He doesn't even think of buying something for himself. These clues and details from the book help me to conclude that Julio is generous and often thinks of others before he thinks of himself. If I can support my conclusions with details from the book as well as from my own experience, I know I've drawn a valid conclusion. As I read on I'll use story clues and my own experience to help me draw conclusions about the characters.

COMPREHENSION CHECK

What surprised you in this part of the book? (Respond to Literature)

What kind of person is Mr. Flores? How do you know? (Key Strategy: Draw Conclusions) *Possible answers: He is respectful to his students and wants to be sure to pronounce their names correctly. We know this because of the way he asks Julio about his name. He wants his students to have fun and learn in new ways. We know this from his assignments.*

Why is Mr. Flores now the teacher for Julio's class? (Cause/Effect) *Possible answer: Mrs. Upchurch left her job, and the school had to hire a new teacher to replace her.*

What parts of Julio's first day of school surprise him? (Summarize)
Possible answer: He finds out that the class is getting a "new" teacher. He learns the class will elect a president.

Do you think Julio enjoyed his first day of school? Explain. (Key Strategy: Draw Conclusions) *Possible answer: He probably enjoyed it. He had fun meeting his pals, and he likes his new teacher.*

Do you think Lucas will agree to run for class president? (Make, Confirm, Revise Predictions) *Possible answer: He probably will agree to do it; the cover of the book shows a poster that says "Elect Lucas for Class President."*

 Think back to your first day in fourth grade or think ahead to your first day in fifth grade. In your Journal describe what the first day of school is like. Who are your classmates? Who is your teacher? What is your classroom like?

Reading On   In the next part of the book (pages 22–41), Julio helps out a classmate during recess. Ask students to predict what might happen, or to set their own purposes for reading.

Reading the Book

Synopsis "What qualities should a good president have?" This is the subject of discussion among the students and the teacher on the second day of class. During recess later that day, Arthur Lewis falls in the soccer game and accidentally breaks his glasses. The children think of ways to help their friend, and Cricket suggests holding a bake sale to raise money to replace the spectacles. Julio escorts Arthur home from school. "I think you'd be a good president for the class," Arthur tells Julio.

COMPREHENSION CHECK

How does the author get readers to care about her characters? (Respond to Literature)

Based on his actions in this part of the book, what conclusions can you come to about Julio? Look back in the book for examples of his behavior. (Key Strategy: Draw Conclusions) *Possible answer: Julio is responsible and thoughtful; he helped Arthur home when Arthur couldn't see well.*

Why do you think Julio wants to be class president? (Make Inferences) *Possible answers: Julio probably thinks he'd do a good job. He might like the attention.*

Think back to the way the author describes Arthur's home. How does being in this setting help Julio learn more about Arthur? (Setting) *Possible answer: Julio learns that Arthur's favorite thing is a clock that runs backward, despite the fact that Arthur has many toys and nice things in his house.*

MINI-LESSON

SETTING

TEACH/MODEL Review what students know about the setting of a story—that it is the time and place of a story. Clues to the time can be found in transportation, clothing, and weather; clues to place in buildings, surroundings, and animals. Discuss the importance of the setting in affecting how characters act and what outcomes to the story are possible.

APPLY Ask students what story details answer the questions "When?" and "Where?" in the opening chapter to this book—what is the setting?

MINI-LESSON

When Arthur's glasses were broken, Julio surprised Arthur by helping him out. Think of a time when someone helped you out when you did not expect it. Write about that time in your Journal. What was the problem? Who helped you? How did this make you feel about that person?

Reading On In the next part of the book (pages 42–65), Julio's class holds its bake sale. Ask students to read on to find out how the sale goes, or to set their own purposes for reading.

S E S S I O N ③

After Pages 42-65

Synopsis The night before the bake sale, Julio and his older brother Nelson, with help from their mother, make brownies from a cake mix. The brownies turn out fine and are a big hit in class the next day. Though the class originally raised the money for Arthur, his glasses were replaced for free. As a result, the fifth-grade class now has $17.40—the proceeds from the sale—to spend on something else.

COMPREHENSION CHECK

What is your favorite scene in this section of the book? (Respond to Literature)

What conclusions can you draw about Nelson based on his behavior in this part of the book? (Key Strategy: Draw Conclusions) *Nelson helps Julio make the brownies and playfully teases him as they work together. This leads to the conclusion that Nelson enjoys doing things with Julio and is always willing to help Julio.*

Do you think Julio will be a good parent when he grows up? Explain (Make Predictions) *Possible answer: Yes, Julio showed kindness, patience, and other good parenting skills when he took care of the twins Marcus and Marius.*

Do you think Julio should have told people he dreamed of being class president? What would you have done? Explain. (Make Judgments) *Possible answer: His classmates might have laughed if he told them. It's probably better that his friend Arthur suggested it. On the other hand, he might have gotten more votes if he had announced it early on. He could have campaigned for votes.*

 Who would you vote for in the election if you were a student in Mr. Flores' class? Explain your answer in your Journal.

Reading On In the next part of the book (pages 66–84), ask students to predict what happens to Julio in the election. Invite them to find out how their predictions compare with the actual events, or to set their own purposes for reading.

SUPPORTING ALL LEARNERS

EXTRA HELP Encourage students to work in collaborative groups to list all the steps the brothers go through to make the brownies. Remind them to look for clue words such as *next, now, and soon* to help them put the steps in order. **(Step by Step)**

CHALLENGE Julio thinks that the picture on the brownie package is misleading because it shows nuts in the brownies and only lists in very small print that nuts are optional. Invite pairs of students to examine ads in magazines and on boxes of products they know well. Have groups work together to compare what the package suggests about the product with what the product is really like. Do they think that the packaging is truthful or is it trying to make the product seem better than it really is? Have them explain their answers. Display their completed work on the bulletin board. **(Make Connections)**

Reading the Book

Synopsis Election day is approaching. The class has learned how to make a nomination, and how to second it. Cricket campaigns for herself by bringing to class a self-promotion poster and distributing candy to classmates. In the meantime, Julio shows good leadership by confronting the school principal about a new school rule. Lucas decides perhaps Julio should run for president after all. Nominations for class president begin and Cricket and Julio vie for the job. Who wins? The candidate who supports others and shows leadership: Julio Sanchez.

COMPREHENSION CHECK

How has Julio changed from the beginning of the story to the end? What do you think of the way he changes? (Respond to Literature)

What caused the principal to change his mind and allow the students to play soccer at recess? (Cause/Effect) *Possible answer: Julio convinces him that soccer is no more dangerous than jumping rope.*

Cricket and Julio are alike in that they both want to be president. What is different about how they behave when they make their statements before the class votes? (Compare/Contrast) *Possible answer: Cricket tries to get Julio disqualifed and tells the class she would be better because she will be president of the United States some day. Julio talks less about what he wants and more about how he will help the class make its own decisions.* MINI-LESSON

What do you think Julio was feeling as the results of the election came in? What makes you say that? (Make Inferences) *Possible answer: Probably happy because he'd been dreaming of winning for quite a while. He feels proud, too.*

What were the reasons Julio won the election? (Key Strategy: Draw Conclusions) *Possible answers: He showed responsibility, leadership, and thoughtfulness. Also, some of the girls in the class voted for him instead of Cricket.*

What do you think Julio should do now that he is class president? In your Journal write a letter to Julio, giving him some advice that could help him do his job well.

MINI-LESSON

COMPARE/CONTRAST

THINK ALOUD When I compare things, I think about how they are alike. When I contrast things, I think about how they are different. I know that both Cricket and Julio want to be class president, but I also know that they are different in many other ways. Understanding how they are different will help me understand why the class picked Julio to be the president. Cricket seems to be more concerned with someday becoming president of the United States than she is with helping the class now. Julio has helped others in the class. I understand why the class decided Julio was better qualified.

APPLY Invite students to use a Venn diagram to record all the ways in which these two characters are alike and different.

(Cricket Julio and Cricket Julio)

Literature Circles

Use these cards to help you as you read and discuss *Class President*.
Record your ideas and answers in your Journal as you read.

SESSION 1
Pages 1-21

TALK ABOUT IT Discuss with your group ways in which "Julio's class" is different from your own. In what ways are they alike? Have each group member record their thoughts about the two classes. Go back to the book for ideas, then discuss. Do these characters and the school setting seem true to life?

SESSION 2
Pages 22-41

TALK ABOUT IT Mr. Flores asks the class what qualities a class president should have. Review the part of the book that contains that discussion. What do you think those qualities should be? Why? Share your views with the rest of the group. Based on what you know about the characters so far, which character in the book, if anyone, has displayed those qualities? In what ways?

SESSION 3
Pages 42-65

TALK ABOUT IT Julio wanted to make brownies for the bake sale. With a partner from your group, discuss how you think Julio felt when he knew he wanted to bring brownies to class but didn't know how to make them. Share your views with the rest of the groups. Did Julio learn from the brownie-making experience? Explain your answers.

SESSION 4
Pages 66-85

TALK ABOUT IT Julio and Cricket had two different approaches to winning the election. What did you think of each approach? Discuss what each candidate could have done to improve his or her chances. If you were their campaign manager, what would you have advised them to do or say differently? Do you think that Cricket would have also been a good class president? Why or why not?

Assess Comprehension

REFLECT AND RESPOND

What do you think author Johanna Hurwitz was trying to say in this book about class elections and leadership? (✔ Theme Connection)

How was the setting important to the story? How might the story be different if it took place at another time? (✔ Setting)

How do you think Julio's family felt about his winning the election? How do you know? (✔ Key Strategy: Draw Conclusions)

How is Julio like Mr. Flores? How are they different? (✔ Compare/Contrast)

STORY ORGANIZER

Copy and distribute the Story Organizer on page 16 of this guide. Invite students to complete this page on their own. Encourage them to share their completed work by comparing their answers with those of other students.

READ CRITICALLY ACROSS TEXTS: CONNECT TO THE SOURCEBOOK

Dinner at Aunt Connie's

◆ Marcy, the narrator in *Dinner at Aunt Connie's*, and Cricket from *Class President* share a goal for the future. They both want to grow up to be president of the United States. Ask students to use what they know about both characters to decide which character might make a better president. Have them give reasons to support their answers.

Trouble at the Mines

◆ Both Mother Jones and Julio spoke up for what they thought was right and inspired others to act. Invite students to discuss the qualities that make Julio and Mother Jones good leaders.

"James Ale"

◆ James Ale was able to convince the mayor to create a new park. Julio was able to convince his principal to allow students to play soccer at recess. These two boys have a lot in common. What advice might James give Julio that would help him with his new job as class president?

A Topic for Conversation

THANK YOU, MR. FLORES

Getting a new teacher leads to big changes for Julio and his classmates. Discuss all the new ideas Mr. Flores brings to his class. Everyone in the class is affected by these changes, but who is affected the most? What is the most important way in which Mr. Flores has changed this student's life?

POSSIBLE ANSWERS:

Julio: He gets to be president of the class! He also learns to have more confidence in himself and to be proud of his heritage.

Cricket: She learns to be nicer to people and she learns that she isn't always the best at everything.

Arthur: He learns how to speak up and that the other students can be his friends.

Lucas: He learns that not everything is based on popularity and having fun.

IDEA FILE

Vocabulary

Instead of using the word *said* after each quote to show who is speaking, Johanna Hurwitz often uses interesting words that help give readers a sense of the person who is speaking. Invite students to use their vocabulary words and a thesaurus to come up with different ways to say *said*. What words would they use if the speaker was happy or excited, sad or angry?

Ask the Author

What questions would students like to ask Johanna Hurwitz? Some students might want to know if Julio or any of the other characters in the book are based on people she knows. Invite students to write their questions in their Journals.

Reviews by You

Is *Class President* a book that students would recommend to a friend? Is it funny? Does it include good ideas about leadership? Encourage students to write their own reviews, including a brief description of the book, and listing reasons why others should or should not read this book.

Campaign Poster

Ask students to think of what they know about Julio, Lucas, and Cricket. Let them pick one of these three as their candidate and create a poster that encourages others to vote for the person they picked. The poster should have a picture, a catchy slogan, and a few sentences that explain why the candidate would make a good president.

Democracy Many nations all over the world hold elections to choose leaders. However, each government follows its own rules for electing leaders. Several hundred years ago the Iroquois people of North America held elections for leaders called *sachems*. Although only a man could become a sachem, only women were allowed to vote. Benjamin Franklin studied the Iroquois system of government when he and others were beginning to write the American constitution. Franklin was impressed by how the five separate tribes of the Iroquois worked together. He hoped that the American states could also work together.

ASSESSMENT

The checked questions on page 12 help assess students' understanding of:

✔ the **theme** of every community having people who lead and inspire others to take action.

✔ the **key strategy** of Drawing Conclusions.

✔ how strategies such as **Compare/Contrast** and **Setting** add to their appreciation of the book.

You may also wish to review and discuss selected students' completed Story Organizers (page 16).

Listen to Students Read Ask selected students to find a place in the book that describes a setting. You may wish to tape-record students as they read the section aloud.

Students may add their recordings, copies of favorite Journal entries, their completed Story Organizer, and other completed assignments to their Literacy Portfolios.

Writing

WRITING PROMPTS

Author's Style: Character

Johanna Hurwitz creates her characters through her descriptions of how they think, how they talk, and how they interact with others. They seem very real. What's her secret? She often bases her characters' actions on things she's seen and heard in real life. Ask students to reread pages 1 and 2 of the book to see how the author introduces Julio by describing his likes and dislikes. Invite students to create a realistic character and describe his or her personality. Remind students to use adjectives to describe the character and examples to show how the character would react in different situations. Encourage students to share their character sketches with partners. What can they add to make the character seem even more realistic?

News Article

Remind students that a good news article answers the questions *Who? What? When? Where?* and *How?* Ask them to imagine that they go to Julio's school and that their job is to write a story about the class election for the school newspaper. Encourage students to pick interesting headings for their stories. Students may wish to use the computer to type their final drafts, using type that makes their articles look like real newspaper articles.

Personal Essay

Mr. Flores asks his class to think about how they would spend a million dollars. Julio thinks of things he would buy for his family. Invite students to consider what they would do with a million dollars. Ask them to list what they would buy and why. Then use these lists to write a personal essay titled "If I had a Million Dollars." Display students' essays on the class bulletin board.

IF I HAD A MILLION DOLLARS.

	What I would Buy	Why
1.		
2.		
3.		
4.		
5.		

Activities

INTEGRATING LANGUAGE ARTS

Writing/Speaking/Listening

Campaign Speech Invite two students to work together. One student will be the candidate for class president, the other will be the campaign manager. Together they should work on a speech for the candidate to give. The speech should tell why the candidate is qualified and what he or she hopes to do as class president. The candidate can deliver the speech to the rest of the class. But first he or she must let the campaign manager contribute ideas and help revise the speech.

Writing/Vocabulary

Create a Poster Julio's class holds a bake sale to earn money to buy Arthur new glasses. Invite students to work together to create posters for the class bake sale. What details do they need to include? What kind of slogan and art work would help catch people's attention? Display completed posters on the bulletin board, and invite the class to discuss what they like best about each one.

INTEGRATING THE CURRICULUM

Science

How Glasses Work Arthur cannot see very well without his glasses. Invite students to research how eyeglasses help people see better. They can use information they find to create diagrams that show how eyeglasses correct faulty vision. Encourage them to create labels for their diagrams and to use the diagrams to help them present on oral report to the rest of the class.

Social Studies

President of the United States Cricket says she's going to run for president of the United States when she grows up. Invite groups of students to work together to come up with top ten lists to show what ten qualities or skills they think someone running for president of the United States should have. Have them carefully copy their list of qualifications onto a poster and display it on the class bulletin board.

Name

Story Organizer

What conclusions have you come to about the characters in *Class President*? Use story clues and what you know to draw conclusions about Julio, Mr. Flores, and Cricket. Use the chart below to record your answers.

Clues From The Story	What I Know	Conclusion
		Julio is
		Mr. Flores is
		Cricket is

Lucas withdrew his name as a candidate and urged others to support Julio. What conclusions can you draw about Lucas and why he did this?